Concrete

by Claire Llewellyn

W
FRANKLIN WATTS

First published in 2002 by
Franklin Watts
96 Leonard Street
London EC2A 4XD

Franklin Watts Australia
56 O'Riordan Street
Alexandria
NSW 2015

Text copyright © Claire Llewellyn 2002

ISBN 0 7496 4269 6

Dewey Decimal
Classification Number: 666

A CIP catalogue record for this book is
available from the British Library

Series editor: Rosalind Beckman
Series designer: James Evans
Picture research: Diana Morris
Photography: Steve Shott

Printed in Hong Kong, China

Acknowledgements

Thanks are due to the following for kind permission to
reproduce photographs:

Allwood-Coppin/Eye Ubiquitous: 27c; Bettmann/Corbis: 12bl;
Jason Burke/Eye Ubiquitous: 18bl; H&H Celcon: 4; CRDPhoto/
Corbis: 15br; Gillian Darley/Edifice/Corbis: 15t; James Davis
Travel Photography: 9bl, 14b, 17bl, 23t; Chris Fairclough/Franklin
Watts Photo Library: 3; Patrick Field/Eye Ubiquitous: 8bl;
V. Kolpakov/Art Directors & Trip PL: 21t; David Langfield/
Eye Ubiquitous: 26b; Darren Maybury/Eye Ubiquitous: 11cr;
Resource Foto/Art Directors & Trip PL: 16b; H. Rogers/
Art Directors & Trip PL: 9tr, 19t; Harmut Schwarzbach/Still
Pictures: 13c; Paul Seheult/Eye Ubiquitous: 11tr; M. Shirley/
Art Directors & Trip PL: 11cl.

Contents

Words printed in **bold italic** are explained in the glossary.

What is concrete?

Concrete is a material that is used for building. It looks and feels a bit like stone. Take a look around and you will see concrete everywhere - it is used to make posts, paths, pavements, roads and buildings.

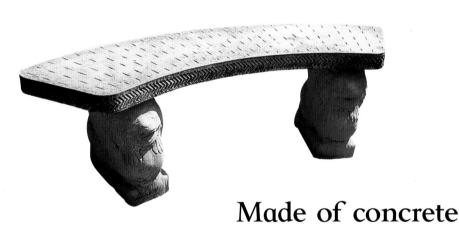

Made of concrete

All the things in these pictures are made of concrete. Can you name them all?

6

Material words

Which of these words describe concrete?

cold   thick   shiny

sticky   stretchy

stiff   solid

heavy

soft   strong

dull

hard

warm

hard-wearing

spongy   light

crisp

colourful

rough   smooth

thin

bendy

slimy

springy

runny

squashy

Take a look

Can you find anything made of concrete in your school or home?

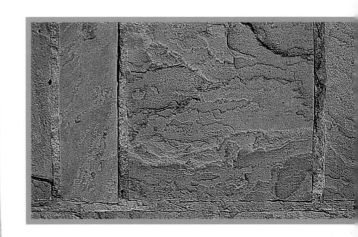

Concrete is strong

Concrete is so strong that it is used in most buildings. But it is also out of sight in the ground. It makes a strong, hard base to put a building on, and keeps posts and poles fixed in the ground.

Standing on concrete

A strong concrete base lies under most kinds of buildings - from garden walls to towering skyscrapers. A building's base is called its *foundations*, and they are very important. Without them, a building would sink into the ground.

These low walls are all you can see of the underground concrete foundations.

Fixed in concrete

Every kind of post needs to be fixed in the ground to stop it toppling over. Flagpoles, fence-posts and the 'legs' of swings and climbing frames are all set in concrete. This makes them strong and safe.

The strong concrete base and posts of this fence stop it falling down.

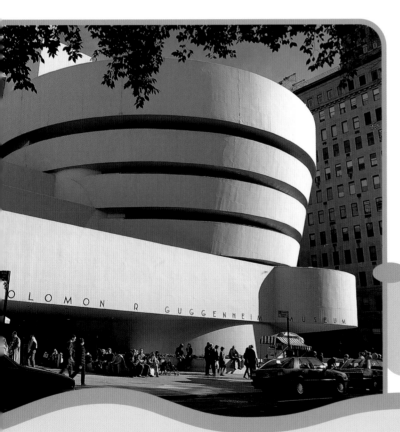

Made of concrete

Many homes, buildings and bridges are made of concrete. The material is so strong that it will stand up to years of bad weather and heavy wear.

Many modern buildings, such as the Guggenheim Museum in New York, are made of concrete because it is so hard-wearing.

Fantastic fact

At 244 m, the Canary Wharf Tower is the UK's tallest building. Its concrete foundations reach 20 m into the ground – that's over six times deeper than the deep end of a swimming pool.

Concrete is smooth and hard-wearing

Concrete is used to make roads, runways, pavements and paths. All these **surfaces** are hard and smooth, and can take a lot of wear.

Smooth walking

In many parts of the world today, the ground we walk on is made of concrete. Every town and city has concrete paths and pavements. The hard surface stands up to the pounding of feet, but is smooth enough for wheelchairs, trolleys and prams.

Concrete pavements are very hard-wearing. They need to last for many years.

Smooth driving

Concrete helps to make a hard, smooth surface for roads and runways. The wheels of cars and trucks can turn quickly and smoothly, giving their drivers a fast and comfortable ride. Aircraft can move at great speed on a hard, flat runway.

Large open spaces made of concrete are perfect for roller-skating and skateboarding!

Huge aircraft take off and land on concrete runways.

Formula 1 racing cars roar along at over 300 kph. The strong concrete race track stands up to the wear.

Take a look

Look at the pavements in your town. What are they made of? How are they made? Why do they sometimes need repairing?

Concrete is waterproof

Concrete is a waterproof material; it will not let water through. That is why concrete is used to make dams, canals and the underground pipes that carry water to and from our homes.

Holding water

Building a dam across a river stops the water flowing to the sea. It forms a huge lake, called a *reservoir*, behind the dam wall. Water is so heavy that dams need to be very strong. Many of them are made of concrete.

The strong concrete wall of a dam stops the water bursting through.

Concrete keeps water in - and out

Huge concrete pipes lie under the streets of every city and town. They are used to deliver clean water to people and carry dirty water away. Concrete is also used to build tunnels beneath rivers and seas. These are used by cars, lorries and trains to transport people and goods from place to place.

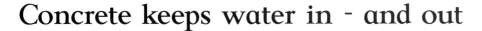

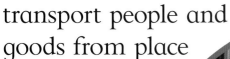

The walls of underwater tunnels are lined with concrete to keep out the water.

Fantastic fact

Nearly 20 million tonnes of concrete were used to build the USA's Grand Coulee dam – the largest concrete dam in the world.

Concrete is long-lasting

Concrete is a kind of **artificial** stone. People have made it for thousands of years. It does not crumble, rot or rust and stands up well to wear. Some of the oldest concrete buildings are still standing today.

Roman 'stone'

Concrete was first used over 2,000 years ago by the Romans. They used the strong, new material in their buildings, bridges and roads, and many of these are still standing today.

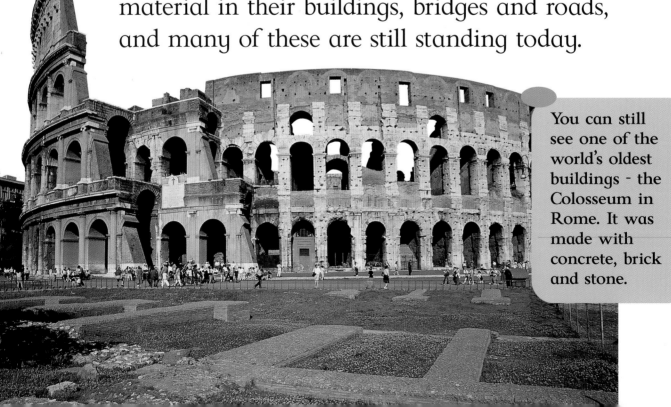

You can still see one of the world's oldest buildings - the Colosseum in Rome. It was made with concrete, brick and stone.

The walls of this concrete bungalow do not need to be painted, but the wooden doors and window frames do.

Easy to care for

Concrete is a material that looks after itself. It does not need oiling, painting or varnishing, or any other kind of care. Concrete does not rust like metal, and it will not rot like wood.

Slow to burn

One of the reasons why concrete buildings last so long is because concrete does not burn well. Unlike buildings made of wood, concrete buildings are slow to burn. Even if they do catch fire, they rarely burn to the ground.

Fantastic fact

Many of the world's most famous buildings are made with concrete. The white tiles on the sails of the Sydney Opera House are stuck to a concrete framework.

Cement is used to make concrete

Concrete is not dug out of the ground. It is made by mixing sand, **gravel** and water with a fine, grey powder called **cement**. The cement makes the mixture stick together, and turns rock-hard when it is dry.

At the quarry

Cement is not a **natural** material; it is produced in factories called cement works. The most important **ingredient** is a rock called **limestone**. Limestone is widely found in the ground. It is dug out of **quarries** and taken to the cement works, where it is crushed into tiny pieces.

Large trucks take the limestone from the quarry to the factories.

At the cement works

The crushed limestone is mixed with clay and water and put in an enormous oven called a **kiln**. There, it is burned in scorching heat. It is then crushed to a fine, dry powder. The cement is packed into strong paper sacks.

Cement can be sold on its own or mixed with sand and gravel in ready-to-use bags.

Fantastic fact

Termites use a kind of cement when they build their 'high-rise' nests (the largest are over 6 m high). They make a soggy mix of sand and saliva that dries hard in the sun.

Concrete is easy to make

Concrete is not difficult to make but, just like baking a cake, it is important to weigh the ingredients with care and mix them together well.

Weigh the ingredients

Making concrete is easy, but the sand, gravel and cement must be carefully weighed and the water must be carefully measured. If too much water is added to the mix, the concrete will crumble and crack.

Concrete is soft and sloppy when wet, but as hard as stone when dry.

Often concrete is mixed in factories and taken to building sites in trucks. A turning drum stops it setting on the way.

Mix with care

It is very important to mix the concrete well so that every grain of sand and gravel is coated with the wet cement. Inside the cement there are chemicals at work, which begin to make the concrete harden. It is important to use the concrete quickly before it begins to **set**.

Try this

Weigh out a little cement mix and place in a small foil or plastic tub. Look at the instructions on the packet. Carefully measure the water and pour it in. Mix well. How long does it take to set?

Wet concrete is poured into moulds

Wet concrete is quick and easy to use. It is poured into a **mould**, pushed down firmly and simply left to harden.

At the building site, a forklift truck carries bucketfuls of cement to different parts of the site.

At the building site

At a large building site, the builders need lorryloads of concrete. The heavy, wet mixture can be pumped through pipes to where it is needed, or transported in tip-up trucks, wheelbarrows or large buckets.

In the mould

Wet concrete is poured into a wooden mould called a *form*. As soon as the form is full, the concrete is pushed down gently to get rid of any pockets of air. It is left for several days to *set*. As it sets, it takes on the shape of the mould.

After the concrete has been poured into the mould, it is pressed down and smoothed on the top.

Quick and easy

Concrete is easier, quicker and cheaper to use than many other building materials. Stone blocks and bricks need to be laid very carefully and are sometimes cut to fit. Concrete can simply be mixed and poured.

Try this

Make your handprint in concrete. Mix some concrete in a hand-sized mould. Now press your hand in the concrete to make a print. Leave to set. Wash your hands as soon as you have finished.

Concrete can be made even stronger

Concrete is a strong material but it can be made even stronger. If steel rods are put inside a mould and wet concrete is poured on top, the concrete hardens around the metal. This makes a material called **reinforced concrete**.

Pushes and pulls

Buildings have to be strong enough to stand up to many *forces*: to pushes and pulls. Concrete is good at standing up to pushes, but it can crack when it is pulled. For buildings, concrete needs to be stronger.

Ordinary concrete sometimes cracks. Reinforced concrete is a stronger material and can move a little without cracking.

Steel and concrete

Just over 100 years ago, someone discovered a way of making concrete stronger. If wet concrete is poured over steel rods, the two materials join together to make a new, much stronger material. This is known as reinforced concrete and is used in most large buildings.

Reinforced concrete is made by pouring wet concrete over steel rods. Can you see the rods sticking out of the concrete columns?

Fantastic fact

Reinforced concrete was invented by a French gardener who wanted to stop his flowerpots breaking. He pushed wire netting inside the wet concrete.

23

Many goods are made of concrete

Concrete is used to make many different items, such as blocks, pipes and paving slabs. Some of these goods are made for builders but others are bought by people who want to use them at home.

Many garden ornaments are made of concrete.

Factory goods

Concrete is not only used at building sites. Factories use it to make bricks, blocks, pipes, paving slabs, wall panels, *girders* and beams. These goods are known as *pre-cast concrete*. They are taken to *builders' merchants*, *DIY shops* and garden centres for builders and other people to buy.

Pre-cast concrete posts can be bought at builders' merchants.

Some concrete blocks are decorated with patterns and used to build a light, airy wall.

Slabs and blocks

Builders use large concrete paving stones to make pavements. Smaller slabs can be used to lay patios or paths. Concrete blocks are bigger than housebricks; it doesn't take long to build a wall with them. Some blocks have holes in them and are decorated with different patterns.

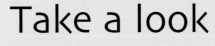

Take a look

Concrete is a much cheaper material than natural stone, but does it look the same? Can you tell which of these paving slabs is made of stone and which is made of concrete?

(The answer is on page 30.)

Concrete and the environment

All around the world people are using more and more concrete - and this is harming the **environment**. Concrete uses a lot of **energy**, causes **pollution** and is very difficult to get rid of.

It takes a lot of energy to dig out the sand from a quarry and transport it to the factory. Quarries also spoil the environment.

Using energy

Making concrete uses a lot of energy. It takes energy to dig out, transport and crush the raw materials. It takes even more energy to heat the cement kiln, which needs to be very hot. Scientists are looking for a way of making cement at cooler temperatures.

Causing pollution

Cement works use a lot of water. The waste water contains harmful substances yet sometimes it is put into rivers and streams. This needs to be carefully controlled. Cement works also pollute the air because they burn so much fuel.

Old buildings produce huge piles of waste concrete. Using the old concrete saves us from producing more.

Making waste

When old concrete buildings are knocked down, they produce huge piles of rubble. Getting rid of the waste concrete can be difficult. One way of using it is to break it up and lay it under car parks and roads. This makes a strong, solid base.

Fantastic fact

In the future, buildings may be made with concrete blocks that fit together like a jigsaw. The blocks could be taken apart and used in another building.

Glossary

Artificial	Not natural; made by people.
Builders' merchants	Shops where builders buy cement, sand and other building materials.
Cement	A fine powder made from limestone that hardens when it is mixed with water. It is an important ingredient of concrete.
Concrete	A hard building material that is made from cement, sand and gravel mixed with water.
DIY shops	Shops where people can buy building materials for use in the home. DIY is short for 'do it yourself'.
Energy	The power that makes machines and living things able to work.
Environment	The world around us, including the land, the air and the sea.
Force	Something that pushes or pulls on a building, making it move.
Form	A wooden mould that is used to hold wet concrete while it sets.
Foundations	The solid concrete base under a building. Foundations are built in holes in the ground to support the building above.

Girder	A strong beam used in building. Girders are used to hold up a floor, road or bridge.
Gravel	A mixture of small stones and sand.
Ingredient	One of a number of things that goes into a mixture.
Kiln	A very hot oven that is used in factories.
Limestone	A kind of rock used to make cement.
Mould	A container with a special shape. Wet concrete is poured into a wooden mould, called a form, to take on its shape.
Natural	Found in the world around us.
Pollution	Spoiling the environment with harmful substances.
Pre-cast concrete	Concrete that has been shaped into pipes, slabs and other items.
Quarry	A place where rocks are dug out of the ground.
Reinforced concrete	A very strong concrete that contains steel rods or wires.
Reservoir	An artificial lake where water is collected and stored.
Set	To become hard and solid.
Surface	The top or outer side.

Index

Answer to question on page 25: The slab on the left is made of concrete; the one on the right is stone.